A LITTLE BOOK OF
WOMEN MYSTICS

A

LITTLE BOOK

OF

Women Mystics

❧

Edited by Carol Lee Flinders

HarperSanFrancisco
A Division of HarperCollins*Publishers*

Permissions acknowledgments begin on page 105
and are a continuation of this copyright page.

Library of Congress Cataloging-in-Publication Data
A little book of women mystics / edited by Carol Lee Flinders. — 1st ed.
p.   cm.
ISBN 0–06–062685–2 (pbk. : alk. paper)
1. Women mystics.   2. Mysticism—Catholic Church—
History—Sources.   I. Flinders, Carol.
BV5080.L5   1995
248.2'2'082—dc20   94–22703

95 96 97 98 99 ❖ HAD 10 9 8 7 6 5 4 3 2

This edition is printed on acid-free paper that meets the American
National Standards Institute Z39.48 Standard.

CONTENTS

INTRODUCTION

Throughout the history of the West, the spiritual experience of women has been marginalized as systematically and as half-consciously as women themselves. The result is a profound thirst, felt now across the whole of our imbalanced culture, for all that has been suppressed. Interest in the women mystics of the European Catholic tradition has never been higher, and for good reason. For when we find our way back to women like Julian of Norwich and Catherine of Siena, who laid hands on the vast richness of the interior life and who challenged the constraints of their time and place to give it voice, the sleeping parts of ourselves begin to stir, and our own spiritual quests are profoundly revitalized.

All true; and yet, how strangely their voices can fall upon our ears. I have wrestled with the problem continually while selecting passages to represent each mystic well and truly. So heavily encoded are their utterances that I keep wanting to intervene, presumptuous as that may be, and explain away the strangeness. When Teresa describes how "the devil," for example, can lead us to overlook the work at hand and reach out for impossible tasks that smack of the heroic, I want to interrupt, "She doesn't mean the devil like with a forked tail and horns, you understand, she's just being figurative and vivid." But who am I to say? And what about Julian's horrendous description of the apparition, long and strangely lean, red like a newly baked tile, who tried to strangle her with his misshapen paws?

No, I think we are the poorer if we downplay too much the elements of their writing that declare the enormous differences between their world and ours. This is why I've kept the devils in—both Teresa's and Julian's—and more, besides.

Contemporary readers, for example, get squeamish when confronted by a bleeding crucifix, whether it's painted above an altar in southern Italy or described in excruciating detail by a visionary poet. We have little feeling for how central Christ's humanity was in medieval devotion—his humanity, and his very flesh. This was a relatively new preoccupation for Christian worshipers, and for women it was of revolutionary significance. Christ's broken, bleeding body, conflated with the triumph of his resurrection and the mystery of redemption, mirrored the central fact of women's lives: as mothers, women literally "incarnate" spirit, bleeding and suffering to give birth, and rejoicing at the outcome. If as Julian tells us Christ really is our mother, "in whom we are endlessly born and out of whom we shall never come," then women have an inside track into his nature and his love.

I hope, therefore, that readers heed the advice of Mechthild ("Nay! Sister! Before all things thou must have breadth of understanding; then only canst thou attain a willing heart and an open soul into which grace may flow") and yield themselves to the potent beauty of these admittedly mysterious writings. What baffles us at the literal level is often, in the deeper recesses of ourselves, just what we are longing to hear.

I'm not sure how to defend my selection of these particular six figures. I do like the breadth they represent of temperament as well as background and calling. I love to imagine them talking together. Of the qualities and preoccupations that unite them, though, one stands out in particular, and this I wish to emphasize.

It seems to me that the hallmark of these women—and perhaps it is the defining characteristic of the mystic in any tradition, male or female—is their profoundly unified attention. Of all the mystics I've included here, Teresa is most explicit on this score. Compelled by the Inquisitors to describe exactly what she means by mental prayer, she speaks of the very first stage, recollection, as a gathering-in of the senses, much as when bees return to the hive. There is nothing forced or harsh in this act; indeed, she says that mental prayer is like conversation between two friends who know and love one another intimately. When *she addresses her nuns at the beginning of* Way of Perfection, *she promises to explain mental prayer to them, but first she spends a long time speaking of essential prerequisites: of the necessity within the sisterhood of mutual love, detachment, and humility. Why? Simply because when any of these ideals is not honored, distractions multiply and real prayer, intensely focused prayer, is impossible.*

Teresa spells it out, but every one of these women lived it out: complete integration of consciousness that informed every act, every gesture, every word, and communicated itself to everyone who came into their presence. Mechthild talks about it in terms of desire, insisting, paradoxically, that desire is our greatest wealth and treasure. When we have come to see that nothing in the finite world can satisfy us and have therefore withdrawn all of our desires from that world, and they are so heavy we can barely support the weight, at that very moment divinity reveals itself. "Give me all that thine is," said God to Mechthild, "and I will give thee all that mine is." And elsewhere, as if standing before a scale, "I have the gold—if you have the weights."

Do we balk, sometimes, at the almost inevitably gendered language with which they speak of God and the soul as man and woman? Perhaps, but cultivating the "breadth" we mentioned above, I think we can suspect that the orthodox language these women used can be seen as just that—a language, stretched to its limits to describe what is by all accounts beyond words. When Catherine of Genoa cries out, "My me is God," her meaning is clear enough.

Finally, we are drawn to these women and their stories, not only by what they appear to have experienced, but by the transformations they were able to work in others and in the world around them. Their strongest claim on our attention, it seems to me, has to do with what we can glean, what we can "translate," if you will, for our own purposes, as we look about our own deeply troubled world and long to begin setting it right.

CHAPTER ONE

Hildegard of Bingen

1098–1179

❧

*T*HE TENTH CHILD *of wealthy, aristocratic parents, Hildegard was offered to God as a "tithe"—a practice not unusual in medieval Europe— when she was just eight years old. A devout family friend* *named Jutta had become a recluse, and to her care the little girl was entrusted as handmaid and spiritual companion. Eventually, their way of life attracted other women, and Jutta established a Benedictine convent. At forty-three, abbess herself by now, Hildegard experienced a "fiery light" and a command to "cry out" on behalf of the church and Christ's teachings. Apocalyptic preacher, composer, poet, healer, administrator, and compiler of scientific lore, Hildegard is not usually described as a mystic, since she says so little about contemplative prayer—a judgment we question when we read her description of "the living light" (the last selection below).*

The excerpts are taken from two sources: Hildegard's *Scivias*, translated by Mother Columba Hart and Jane Bishop (New York: Paulist Press, 1990); and *Symphonia*, translated and edited by Barbara Newman (Ithaca, NY: Cornell University Press, 1988).

*W*HEN I WAS forty-two years and seven months old, Heaven was opened and a fiery light of exceeding brilliance came and permeated my whole brain, and inflamed my whole heart and my whole breast, nor like a burning but like a warming flame, as the sun warms anything its rays touch. And immediately I knew the meaning of the exposition of the Scriptures. . . . I had sensed in myself wonderfully the power and mystery of secret and admirable visions from my childhood—that is, from the age of five—up to that time, as I do now. This, however, I showed to no one except a few religious persons who were living in the same manner as I; but meanwhile, until the time when God by His grace wished it to be manifested, I concealed it in quiet silence. But the visions I saw I did not perceive in dreams, or sleep, or delirium, or by the eyes of the body, or by the ears of the outer self, or in hidden places; but I received them while awake and seeing with a pure mind and the eyes and ears of the inner self, in open places, as God willed it. . . .

But when I had passed out of childhood and had reached the age of full maturity mentioned above, I heard a voice from Heaven saying, "I am the Living Light, Who illuminates the darkness. The person whom I have chosen and whom I have miraculously stricken as I willed, I have placed among great wonders. . . .

"Oh, human, who receives these things meant to manifest what is hidden not in the disquiet of deception but in the purity of simplicity, write, therefore, the things you see and hear."

But I, though I saw and heard these things, refused to write for a long time through doubt and bad opinion and the diversity of human words, not with stubbornness but in the exercise of humility, until laid low by the scourge of God, I fell upon a bed of sickness; then, compelled at last by many illnesses . . . I set my hand to the writing. . . .

And I spoke and wrote these things not by the invention of my heart or of that of any other person, but as by the secret mysteries of God I heard and received them in the heavenly places.

And again I heard a voice from Heaven saying to me, "Cry out therefore, and write thus!"

(SCIVIAS 59)

FOR THE WILL is like a fire, baking each deed as if in a furnace. Bread is baked so that people may be nourished by it and be able to live. So too the will is the strength of the whole work, for it starts by kneading it and when it is firm adds the yeast and pounds it severely; and thus, preparing the work in contemplation as if it were bread, it bakes it in perfection by the full action of its ardor, and so makes a greater food for humans in the work they do than in the bread they eat. A person stops eating from time to time, but the work of his will goes on in him till his soul leaves his body. And

in whatever differing circumstances the work is per-
formed . . . it always progresses in the will and in the
will comes to perfection.

(PART 1, VISION 4, NUMBER 21;

SCIVIAS 121–22)

A ND I, a person not glowing with the strength of
strong lions or taught by their inspiration, but a
tender and fragile rib imbued with a mystical breath,
saw a blazing fire, incomprehensible, inextinguishable,
wholly living and wholly Life, with a flame in it the
color of the sky, which burned ardently with a gentle
breath, and which was as inseparably within the blazing
fire as the viscera are within a human being.

(2.1.1; *SCIVIAS* 149)

RESPLENDENT JEWEL and unclouded brightness
of the sunlight streaming through you,
know that the sun is a fountain leaping
from the father's heart,
his all-fashioning word.
He spoke and the primal matrix
teemed with things unnumbered—
but Eve unsettled them all.

To you the father spoke again
but this time
the word he uttered was a man
in your body.
Matrix of light! through you he breathed forth
all that is good,
as in the primal matrix he formed
all that has life.

(SYMPHONIA 115)

BECAUSE IT WAS a woman
who built a house for death
a shining girl tore it down.
So now
when you ask for blessings
seek the supreme one
in the form of a woman
surpassing all that God made
since in her
(O tender! O blessed!)
he became one of us.

(117)

ALLELUIA! LIGHT
burst from your untouched
womb like a flower
on the farther side
of death. The world-tree
is blossoming. Two
realms become one.

(125)

SONG TO THE VIRGIN

NEVER WAS LEAF SO green,
for you branched from the spirited
blast of the quest
of the saints.

When it came time
for your boughs to blossom
(I salute you!)
your scent was like balsam
distilled in the sun.
And your flower made all spices
fragrant
dry though they were:
they burst into verdure.

So the skies rained dew on the grass
and the whole earth exulted,
for her womb brought forth wheat,
for the birds of heaven
made their nests in it.

Keepers of the feast, rejoice!
The banquet's ready. And you
sweet maid-child
are a fount of gladness.

But Eve?
She despised every joy.
Praise nonetheless,
Praise to the Highest.

(127)

ANTIPHON FOR THE HOLY SPIRIT

THE SPIRIT OF GOD
is a life that bestows life,
root of the world-tree
and wind in its boughs.
Scrubbing out sins,
she rubs oil into wounds.

She is glistening life
alluring all praise,
all-awakening,
all-resurrecting.

(141)

IN THIS VISION my soul, as God would have it, rises up high into the vault of heaven and into the changing sky and spreads itself out among different peoples, although they are far away from me in distant lands and places. And because I see them this way in my soul, I observe them in accord with the shifting of clouds and other created things. I do not hear them with my outward ears, nor do I perceive them by the thoughts of my own heart or by any combination of my five senses, but in my soul alone, while my outward eyes are open. So I have never fallen prey to ecstasy in the visions, but I see them wide awake, day and night. . . . The light that I see thus is not spatial, but it is far, far brighter than a cloud that carries the sun. I can measure neither height, nor length, nor breadth in it; and I call it "the reflection of the living Light." And as the sun, the moon, and the stars appear in water, so writings, sermons, virtues, and certain human actions take form for me and gleam within it.

Now whatever I have seen or learned in this vision remains in my memory for a long time, so that, when I have seen and heard it, I remember; and I see, hear, and know all at once, and as if in an instant I learn what I know. But what I do not see, I do not know, for I am not educated. . . . And the words in this vision are not like words uttered by a human mouth, but like a shimmering flame, or a cloud floating in a clear sky.

Moreover, I can no more recognize the form of this light than I can gaze directly on the sphere of the sun. Sometimes—but not often—I see within this light another light, which I call "the living Light." And I cannot describe when and how I see it, but while I see it all sorrow and anguish leave me, so that then I feel like a simple girl instead of an old woman.

(LETTER, CITED IN
SCIVIAS INTRODUCTION, 18–19)

CHAPTER TWO

Mechthild of Magdeburg

1210–1297

❦

*M*ECHTHILD TELLS US *she experienced her first "greeting from God" when she was only twelve. She left home at about twenty-three to pursue her religious vocation in the city of Magdeburg. There she was* affiliated with the Beguines, that remarkable "order that was no order," which originated in Belgium and spread through much of Germany and France in the thirteenth century. Late in life, broken by illness and by conflicts with other religious—probably the "cathedral clergy" whose corrupt lifestyle she rebuked—she was invited to live at a Benedictine convent at Helfta, where she enjoyed the companionship of some of the great women mystics of the age. The first European mystic to write in vernacular German, Mechthild drew heavily upon the courtly love tradition to describe her experiences.

The excerpts are all from *The Flowing Light of the Godhead*, by Mechthild of Magdeburg, translated by Lucy Menzies (Glasgow, Scotland: Wild Goose Publications, 1953).

*T*HE TRUE GREETING of God, which comes from the heavenly flood out of the spring of the flowing Trinity, has such power that it takes all strength from the body and lays the soul bare to itself. Thus it sees itself as one of the blessed and receives in itself divine glory. The soul is thus separated from the body with its power and love and longing. Only the smallest part of life remains to the body which is as it were in a sweet sleep. . . . And He clothes it with such garments as are worn in His palace and girds it with strength. Then it may ask for what it will, it will be granted to it.

Should it not be granted, it is because the soul is taken further by God to a secret place where it must not ask nor pray for anyone, for God alone will play with it in a game of which the body knows nothing. . . . Thus God and the soul soar further to a blissful place of which I neither can nor will say much.

(*FLOWING LIGHT* 6)

OUR LORD DELIGHTS in Heaven
Because of the loving soul He has on earth,
And says, "Look how she who has wounded Me
    has risen!
. . . And comes racing like a hunted deer
To the spring which is Myself.
She comes soaring like an eagle
Swinging herself from the depths
Up into the heights."

GOD

Thou huntest sore for thy love,
What bring'st thou Me, my Queen?

SOUL

Lord! I bring Thee my treasure;
It is greater than the mountains,
Wider than the world,

Deeper than the sea,
Higher than the clouds,
More glorious than the sun,
More manifold than the stars,
It outweighs the whole earth!

GOD

O thou! image of my divine godhead,
Ennobled by my humanity,
Adorned by my holy spirit,
What is thy treasure called?

SOUL

Lord! It is called my heart's desire!
I have withdrawn it from the world,
Denied it to myself and all creatures.
Now I can bear it no longer.
Where, O Lord, shall I lay it?

Thy heart's desire shalt thou lay nowhere
But in mine own divine heart
And on my human breast.
There alone wilt thou find comfort
And be embraced by my spirit.

(18–20)

I CANNOT DANCE, O Lord, unless thou lead me.
If thou wilt that I leap joyfully
Then must thou thyself first dance and sing!
Then will I leap for love
From love to knowledge,
From knowledge to fruition,
From fruition to beyond all human sense.
There will I remain
And circle evermore.

(21)

FISH CANNOT DROWN in the water,
 Birds cannot sink in the air,
Gold cannot perish
In the refiner's fire.
This has God given to all creatures
To foster and seek their own nature,
How then can I withstand mine?
I must to God—
My father through nature,
my brother through humanity,
My bridegroom through love,
His am I forever!
Think ye that fire must utterly slay my soul?
NAY! Love can both fiercely scorch
And tenderly love and console.

(24)

THEN OUR LORD said—
Stand, O soul!

SOUL

What wilt thou, Lord?

THE LORD

Thy self must go!

SOUL

But Lord, what shall happen to me, then?

THE LORD

Thou art by nature already mine!
Nothing can come between Me and thee!
There is no angel so sublime
As to be granted for one hour
What is given thee for ever.

Therefore must thou put from thee
Fear and shame and all outward things.
Only of that of which thou art sensible by nature
Shalt thou wish to be sensible in eternity.
That shall be thy noble longing,
Thine endless desire,
And that in my infinite mercy
I will evermore fulfill.

SOUL

Lord! Now am I a naked soul
And thou a God most glorious!
Our two-fold intercourse is love eternal
Which can never die.
Now comes a blessed stillness
Welcome to both. He gives himself to her
And she to him.
What shall now befall her, the soul knows:

Therefore am I comforted.
Where two lovers come secretly together
They must often part, without parting.

(25)

THERE IS NO LORD in all the world
Who lives in all his dwellings at once
Save God alone.
He lives in the peace of holy love
And whispers with his love
In the narrow confines of the soul.

(50)

OF THE HEAVENLY THINGS God has shown me
I can speak but a little word,
Not more than a honey-bee
Can carry away on its foot
From an over-flowing jar. . . .

(67)

Wouldst thou come with me to the wine-cellar,
That will cost thee much;
Even hadst thou a thousand marks
It were all spent in one hour!
If thou wouldst drink the unmingled wine
Thou must ever spend more than thou hast,
And the host will never fill thy glass to the brim!
Thou wilt become poor and naked,
Despised of all who would rather see themselves
In the dust, than squander their all in the wine-cellar.
This also thou must suffer,
That thy friends look askance at thee
Who go with thee to the inn.
How greatly they will scorn thee
When they cannot dare such costs
But must have water mixed with wine.

(70)

A H, DEAR LORD! How poor I was that I could neither think of all these words, nor pray, nor love! Then I crept to thee and said: "Lord! wherewith can I honour thee now? . . ." Then my Love spake: "I will set a light in the lantern and a special ray of understanding shall shine into every eye that sees the light!" Then the soul asked in great humility, yet without fear: "Beloved! What shall that lantern be?"

And our Lord answered: "I am the light! Thy breast is the lantern!"

(80)

I, UNWORTHY SINNER, was greeted so overpoweringly by the Holy Spirit in my twelfth year when I was alone, that I could no longer have given way to any serious daily sin. The loving greeting came every day and caused me both love and sorrow; the sweetness and glory increased daily and this continued for thirty-one years.

I knew nothing of God except the usual Christian beliefs and I tried to follow them diligently that my heart might become pure. God himself is my witness that I never consciously asked him to give me the things of which I have written in this book. I had never dreamt that such things could come to any human being.

(94–95)

I CANNOT WRITE nor do I wish to write—but I see this book with the eyes of my soul and hear it with the ears of my eternal spirit and feel in every part of my body the power of the Holy Spirit.

(108)

IF THOU GIVEST GOD all that thine is, within and without, God will truly give thee all that His is, within and without.

(110)

*T*HAT PRAYER has great power which a person makes with all his might. It makes a sour heart sweet, a sad heart merry, a poor heart rich, a foolish heart wise, a timid heart brave, a sick heart well, a blind heart full of sight, a cold heart ardent.

It draws down the great God into the little heart, it drives the hungry soul up into the fullness of God, it brings together two lovers, God and the soul in a wondrous place where they speak much of love.

(136)

*W*OULDST THOU KNOW my meaning?
Lie down in the Fire
See and taste the flowing
Godhead through thy being;
Feel the holy spirit
Moving and compelling

Thee within the flowing
Fire and light of God.

(194)

WHAT CAN BE SEEN with human eyes, heard by
human ears and spoken by the human tongue, is
as different from the truth revealed to the loving soul as
a wax candle to the full sun.

(199)

SEE THERE WITHIN the flesh
Like a bright wick, englazed
The soul God's finger lit
To give her liberty
And joy and power and love,
To make her crystal, like
As maybe, to Himself.

(209)

OUR CHILDHOOD was foolish, our youth troubled; how we conquered it is known only to God. Alas now in my old age I find much to chide, for it can produce no shining works and is cold and without grace. It is powerless, now that it no longer has youth to help it to bear the fiery love of God. . . . Seven years ago a troubled old soul lamented these weaknesses to our Lord. God answered thus: "Thy childhood was a companion of my holy spirit; thy youth was a bride of my humanity; in thine old age thou art a humble house-wife of my Godhead."

(212)

EVER LONGING in the soul
Ever suffering in the body,
Ever pain in the senses
Ever hope in the heart in Jesus alone—

Those who have given themselves utterly to God
Know well what I mean.

(260)

AH! BELOVED PRISON
In which I have been bound,
I thank thee for all
In which thou hast followed me.
Though I have often been troubled by thee,
Yet didst thou oft come to my aid.
All thy need will yet be taken from thee
At the last Day—
Therefore we will lament no more
But will be filled with gladness
For all that God has done to us both.
Now let us only stand fast
In sweet hope!

(263)

CHAPTER THREE

Julian of Norwich

1342–1416

✖

AN ANCHORESS *whose cell adjoined the parish church of St. Julian in Conisford at Norwich, Julian may not yet have been so enclosed in May 1373, when she witnessed a series of sixteen divine revelations* curred over a twenty-four-hour period. She described these in what is now called the Short Text of her Showings, but about twenty years later she described them again, amplifying her account to nearly three times the original length. For two things in particular contemporary seekers are deeply grateful to Julian: First, she reported that in none of her visions did she see any evidence that God is wrathful. Of hell and purgatory, for that matter, "I saw nothing." Second, she discovered that maternality is as intrinsic to God's nature as majesty.

The excerpts are all from *Julian of Norwich: Showings*, edited by Edmund Colledge, O.S.A., and James Walsh, S.J. (New York: Paulist Press, 1978).

I SAW THAT HE is to us everything which is good and comforting for our help. He is our clothing, who wraps and enfolds us for love, embraces us and shelters us, surrounds us for his love, which is so tender that he may never desert us. . . . And in this he showed me something small, no bigger than a hazelnut, lying in the palm of my hand, as it seemed to me, and it was as round as a ball. I looked at it with the eye of my understanding and thought: what can this be? I was amazed that it could last, for I thought that because of its littleness it would suddenly have fallen into nothing. And I was answered in my understanding: It lasts and always will, because God loves it; and thus everything has being through the love of God.

(183)

GOD, OF YOUR GOODNESS give me yourself, for you are enough for me, and I can ask for nothing which is less which can pay you full worship. And if I ask anything which is less, always I am in want: but only in you do I have everything.

(184)

T HE GREAT DROPS of blood fell from beneath the crown like pellets, looking as if they came from the veins, and as they issued they were a brownish red, for the blood was very thick, and as they spread they turned bright red. And as they reached the brows they vanished; and even so the bleeding continued until I had seen and understood many things. Nevertheless, the beauty and the vivacity persisted, beautiful and vivid without diminution.

The copiousness resembles the drops of water which fall from the eaves of a house after a great shower of rain, falling so thick that no human ingenuity can count them. And in their roundness as they spread over the forehead they were like a herring's scales. . . . This vision was living and vivid and hideous and fearful and sweet and lovely. . . .

(187–88)

O NCE MY UNDERSTANDING was let down into the bottom of the sea, and there I saw green hills and valleys, with the appearance of moss strewn with seaweed and gravel. Then I understood in this way: that if a man or woman were there under the wide waters, if he could see God, as God is continually with man, he would be safe in soul and body, and come to no harm.

(193)

I OFTEN WONDERED WHY, through the great prescient wisdom of God, the beginning of sin was not prevented. For then it seemed to me that all would have been well.

. . . But Jesus, who in this vision informed me about everything needful to me, answered with these words and said: Sin is necessary, but all will be well, and all will be well, and every kind of thing will be well.

(224–25)

I DID NOT SEE SIN, for I believe that it has no kind of substance, no share in being, nor can it be recognized except by the pain caused by it.

(225)

A ND THIS IS a supreme friendship of our courteous Lord, that he protects us so tenderly whilst we are in our sins; and furthermore he touches us most secretly, and shows us our sins by the sweet light of mercy and grace. But when we see ourselves so foul, then we believe that God may be angry with us because of our sins. Then we are moved by the Holy Spirit through contrition to prayer, and we desire with all our might an amendment of ourselves to appease God's anger, until the time that we find rest of soul and ease of conscience. And then we hope that God has forgiven us our sin; and this is true. And then our courteous Lord shows himself to the soul, happily and with the gladdest countenance, welcoming it as a friend, as if it had been in pain and in prison, saying: My dear darling, I am glad that you have come to me in all your woe. I have always been with you, and now you see me loving, and we are made one in bliss.

(246)

*P*RAYER UNITES THE SOUL to God, for though the soul may be always like God in nature and in substance restored by grace, it is often unlike him in condition, through sin on man's part. Then prayer is a witness that the soul wills as God wills, and it eases the conscience and fits man for grace. And so he teaches us to pray and to have firm trust that we shall have it; for he beholds us in love, and wants to make us partners in his good will and work.

(253)

A ND SO WE SHALL by his sweet grace in our own meek continual prayer come into him now in this life by many secret touchings of sweet spiritual sights and feelings, measured out to us as our simplicity may bear it. And this is done and will be done by the grace of the Holy Spirit, until the day that we die, still longing for love. And then we shall all come into our Lord, knowing ourselves clearly and wholly possessing God, and we shall all be endlessly hidden in God, truly seeing and wholly feeling, and hearing him spiritually and delectably smelling him and sweetly tasting him. And there we shall see God face to face, familiarly and wholly.

(255)

B**UT OUR PASSING LIFE** which we have here does not know in our senses what our self is, but we know in our faith. And when we know and see, truly and clearly, what our self is, then we shall truly and clearly see and know our Lord God in the fullness of joy.

(258)

I **SAW NO KIND OF WRATH** in God, neither briefly nor for long. For truly, as I see it, if God could be angry for any time, we should neither have life nor place nor being . . . for though we may feel in ourselves anger, contention and strife, still we are all mercifully enclosed in God's mildness and in his meekness, in his benignity and in his accessibility. . . .

(264–65)

IN THIS ENDLESS LOVE we are led and protected by God, and we never shall be lost; for he wants us to know that the soul is a life, which life of his goodness and his grace will last in heaven without end, loving him, thanking him, praising him. And just as we were to be without end, so we were treasured and hidden in God, known and loved from without beginning. . . . And furthermore, he wants us to know that this beloved soul was preciously knitted to him in its making, by a knot so subtle and so mighty that it is united in God.

(284)

AND I SAW no difference between God and our substance, but, as it were, all God; and still my understanding accepted that our substance is in God. . . . For the almighty truth of the Trinity is our Father, for he made us and keeps us in him. And the deep wisdom of the Trinity is our Mother, in whom we are enclosed. And the high goodness of the Trinity is our Lord, and in him we are enclosed and he in us.

(285)

OUR MOTHER in nature, our Mother in grace, because he wanted altogether to become our Mother in all things, made the foundation of his work most humbly and most mildly in the maiden's womb.... The mother's service is nearest, readiest and surest: nearest because it is most natural, readiest because it is most loving, and surest because it is truest. No one ever might or could perform this office fully, except only for him. We know that all our mothers bear us for pain and for death. O, what is that? But our true Mother Jesus, he alone bears us for joy and for endless life, blessed may he be. So he carries us within him in love and travail, until the full time when he wanted to suffer the sharpest thorns and cruel pains that ever were or will be, and at the last he died. . . .

The mother can give her child to suck of her milk, but our precious Mother Jesus can feed us with himself, and does, most courteously and most tenderly, with the blessed sacrament, which is the precious food of true life. . . .

The mother can lay her child tenderly to her breast, but our tender Mother Jesus can lead us easily into his blessed breast through his sweet open side, and show us there a part of the godhead and of the joys of heaven, with inner certainty of endless bliss. . . .

This fair lovely word "mother" is so sweet and so kind in itself that it cannot truly be said of anyone or to anyone except of him and to him who is the true Mother of life and of all things.

(297–99)

A<small>ND THEREFORE</small> it is a certain thing, good and gracious to will, meekly and fervently, to be fastened and united to our mother Holy Church, who is Christ Jesus. For the flood of mercy which is his dear blood and precious water is plentiful to make us fair and clean. The blessed wounds of our saviour are open and rejoice to heal us. The sweet gracious hands of our Mother are ready and diligent about us.

(287)

A<small>ND AS SOON</small> as I fell asleep, it seemed to me that the devil set himself at my throat, thrusting his face, like that of a young man, long and strangely lean, close to mine. I never saw anything like him; his colour was red, like a newly baked tile, with black spots like freckles, uglier than a tile. His hair was red as rust, not cut short in front, with side-locks hanging at his temples. He grinned at me with a vicious look, showing me white teeth so big that it all seemed the uglier to me. His body and his hands were mis-shapen, but he held me by the throat with his paws, and wanted to stop my breath and kill me, but he could not.

(311–12)

AND THEN OUR GOOD Lord opened my spiritual eye, and showed me my soul in the midst of my heart. I saw the soul as wide as if it were an endless citadel, and also as if it were a blessed kingdom, and from the state which I saw in it, I understood that it is a fine city. In the midst of that city sits our Lord Jesus, true God and true man. . . .

(312–13)

SOME OF US BELIEVE that God is almighty and may do everything, and that he is all wisdom and can do everything, but that he is all love and wishes to do everything, there we fail. And it is this ignorance which most hinders God's lovers, as I see it; for when we begin to hate sin and to amend ourselves according to the laws of Holy Church, there still persists a fear which hinders us, by looking at ourselves and at our sins committed in the past, and some of us because of our everyday sins, because we do not keep our promise or keep the purity which God has established us in, but often fall into so much wretchedness that it is shameful to say it. And the perception of this makes us so woebegone and so depressed that we can scarcely see any consolation. And sometimes we take this fear for humility, but it is a reprehensible blindness and weakness. . . .

(323)

A S TO THE PENANCE which one takes upon oneself, that was not revealed to me. . . . But what was revealed, specially and greatly and in a most loving manner, is that we ought meekly and patiently to bear and suffer the penance which God himself gives us, with recollection of his blessed Passion. . . .

For he says: Do not accuse yourself that your tribulation and your woe is all your fault; for I do not want you to be immoderately depressed or sorrowful. For I tell you that whatever you do, you will have woe. And therefore I want you wisely to understand the penance which you are continually in, and to accept that meekly for your penance. And then you will truly see that all your life is profitable penance.

This place is prison, this life is penance, and he wants us to rejoice in the remedy.

The remedy is that our Lord is with us, protecting us and leading us into the fullness of joy. . . .

(330–31)

CHAPTER FOUR

Catherine of Siena

1347–1380

❦

DAUGHTER OF A *Sienese wool dyer, twenty-fourth of twenty-five children, Catherine Benincasa lived only thirty-three years, but within that short lifetime she established herself as one of the greatest* *mystics of her age. She was not a cloistered nun but rather a member of the Dominican Third Order (laypeople whose lives are dedicated to prayer and service in the spirit of the order's founder). Her extraordinary prophetic and visionary gifts allowed her to combat the ills of the Catholic Church, which were considerable, on every level. Her devoted followers, the Caterinati, came from all social classes, including the church authorities she held most responsible for the widespread corruption that had finally culminated in the Great Schism. Most of Catherine's writings, aside from the letters, were dictated during ecstatic states. The excerpts taken from her* Dialogue, *it should be noted, are not in Catherine's own voice: God is speaking in most cases, though sometimes the voice belongs to a kind of omniscient narrator.*

The citations are from *The Dialogue*, translated by Suzanne Noffke, O.P. (New York: Paulist Press, 1980); *Letters*, translated by Suzanne Noffke, O.P. (Binghamton, NY: Medieval and Renaissance Texts and Studies,

1988); *The Life of St. Catherine of Siena,* by Raymond of Capua, translated by George Lamb (Chicago: P. J. Kenedy & Sons, 1960); and *Prayers,* translated by Suzanne Noffke, O.P. (New York: Paulist Press, 1983).

A SOUL RISES UP, restless with tremendous desire for God's honor and the salvation of souls. She has for some time exercised herself in virtue and has become accustomed to dwelling in the cell of self-knowledge in order to know better God's goodness toward her, since upon knowledge follows love. And loving, she seeks to pursue truth and clothe herself in it.

But there is no way she can so savor and be enlightened by this truth as in continual humble prayer, grounded in the knowledge of herself and of God. For by such prayer the soul is united with God, following in the footsteps of Christ crucified, and through desire and affection and the union of love he makes of her another himself.

(*DIALOGUE 25*)

S HE FOUND HERSELF eager for the next day's Mass—it would be Mary's day—because in communion the soul seems more sweetly bound to God and better knows his truth. For then the soul is in God and God in the soul, just as the fish is in the sea and the sea in the fish.

(27)

I HAVE SHOWN YOU, dearest daughter, that in this life guilt is not atoned for by any suffering simply as suffering, but rather by suffering borne with desire, love, and contrition of heart. The value is not in the suffering but in the soul's desire. . . .

You ask me for suffering to atone for the offenses my creatures commit against me. And you ask for the will to know and love me, supreme Truth. Here is the way, if you would come to perfect knowledge and enjoyment of me, eternal Life: Never leave the knowledge of yourself. Then, put down as you are in the valley of humility

you will know me in yourself, and from this knowledge
you will draw all that you need.

(29)

VIRTUE, ONCE CONCEIVED, must come to birth.
Therefore, as soon as the soul has conceived through
loving affection, she gives birth for her neighbor's sake.
And just as she loves me in truth, so also she serves her
neighbors in truth. Nor could she do otherwise, for love
of me and love of neighbor are one and the same thing:
Since love of neighbor has its source in me, the more the
soul loves me, the more she loves her neighbors.

(36–37)

VIRTUE CANNOT BE PERFECT or bear fruit
except by means of your neighbors. If a
woman has conceived a child but never brings it to
birth for people to see, her husband will consider

himself childless. Just so, I am the spouse of the soul, and unless she gives birth to the virtue she has conceived [by showing it] in her charity to her neighbors in their general and individual needs in the ways I have described, then I insist that she has never in truth even conceived virtue within her.

(45)

A S THE SOUL comes to know herself she also knows God better, for she sees how good he has been to her. In the gentle mirror of God she sees her own dignity: that through no merit of hers but by his creation she is the image of God. And in the mirror of God's goodness she sees as well her own unworthiness, the work of her own sin. For just as you can better see the blemish on your face when you look at yourself in a mirror, so the soul who in true self-knowledge rises up with desire to look at herself in the gentle mirror of God with the eye of understanding sees all the more clearly her own defects because of the purity she sees in him.

Now as light and knowledge grew more intense in this soul, a sweet bitterness was both heightened and mellowed. The hope that first Truth has given her mellowed it. But as a flame burns higher the more fuel is fed it, the fire in this soul grew so great that her body could not have contained it. She could not, in fact, have survived had she not been encircled by the strength of him who is strength itself.

(48)

WHEN MY SON was lifted up on the wood of the most holy cross he did not cut off his divinity from the lowly earth of your humanity. So though he was raised so high he was not raised off the earth. In fact, his divinity is kneaded into the clay of your humanity like one bread.

(65)

ALL SUFFERING in this life is small with the smallness of time. Time is no more than the point of a needle, and when time is over, so is suffering.

(93)

PERFECT PRAYER is achieved not with many words but with loving desire, when the soul rises up to me with knowledge of herself, each movement seasoned by the other. In this way she will have vocal and mental prayer at the same time, for the two stand together like the active and contemplative life. Still, vocal and mental prayer are understood in many different ways. This is why I told you that holy desire, that is, having a good and holy will, is continual prayer. . . . Whatever you do in word or deed for the good of your neighbor is a real prayer. (I am assuming that you actually pray as such at the appointed time.)

(126)

In this mortal life, so long as you are pilgrims, I have bound you with the chain of charity. Whether you want it or not, you are so bound. If you should break loose by not wanting to live in charity for your neighbors, you will still be bound by it by force. Thus, that you may practice charity in action and in will, I in my providence did not give to any one person or to each individually the knowledge for doing everything necessary for human life. No, I gave something to one, something else to another, so that each one's need would be a reason to have recourse to the other.

(311)

[Told to her confessor after a visionary experience during which Christ and she had exchanged hearts:]

Can't you see, Father, that I am not the person I was, but am changed into someone else? If only you could understand how I feel, Father! . . . My mind is so full of joy and happiness that I am amazed my soul stays in my body. There is so much heat in my soul that this material fire seems cool by comparison, rather than to be giving out heat; it seems to have gone out, rather than to be still burning. This heat has generated in my mind a renewal of purity and humility, so that I seem to have gone back to the age of four or five. And at the same time so much love of my fellow-men has blazed up in me that I could face death for them cheerfully and with great joy in my heart."

(LIFE 167)

[To one of her confessors:]

I, CATERINA, servant and slave of the servants of Jesus Christ, am writing to encourage you in the precious blood of God's Son. I long to see you set afire, swallowed up and consumed in his blazing charity, for we know that those who are set afire and consumed in that true charity lose all self-consciousness. That is what I want you to do.

I am inviting you, in this blazing charity, to plunge into a peaceful sea, a deep sea. I have just rediscovered the sea—not that the sea is new, but it is new to me in the way my soul experiences it—in the words, "God is love." And just as a mirror reflects a person's face and as the sun shines its light on the earth, so these words echo within me that everything that is done is simply love, because everything is made entirely of love.

(LETTER 27)

TRULY THE SOUL'S being united with and transformed into him is like fire consuming the dampness in logs. Once the logs are heated through and through, the fire burns and changes them into itself, giving them its own color and warmth and power. It is just so with us when we look at our Creator and his boundless charity. We begin to experience the heat of self-knowledge—which consumes all the dampness of our selfish love for ourselves. As the heat increases, we throw ourselves with blazing desire into God's measureless goodness, which we discover within our very selves. We are then sharing in his warmth and in his power, in that we begin at once to feed on and savor souls. . . .

(LETTER 45)

THE HUMAN HEART is drawn by love as by nothing else, since it is made of love. This seems to be why human beings love so much, because they are made of nothing but love, body and soul. In love God created them in his own image and likeness, and in love father and mother conceive and bring forth their children, giving them a share in their own substance. So God, seeing that humankind is so quick to love, throws out to us right away the hook of love, giving us the Word, his only-begotten Son. He takes on our humanity to make a great peace.

(LETTER 64)

LOVE, LOVE, LOVE one another! Be glad, be jubilant! Summertime is coming! For on the night of April first God disclosed his secrets more than usual. He showed his marvels in such a way that my soul seemed to be outside my body and was so overwhelmed with joy that I can't really describe it in words. He told and explained bit by bit the mystery of the persecution holy Church is now enduring, and of the renewal and exaltation to come. He said that what is happening now is being permitted to restore her to her original condition. . . .

(LETTER 65)

[To her mother, in Siena, when Catherine had been detained in Avignon:]

DEAREST MOTHER ... How I have longed to see you truly the mother of my soul as well as of my body! For I know that if you love my soul more than you love my body, any excessive attachment you may have will die, and my physical absence won't be so wearing on you. No, it will even bring you consolation, and you will be ready to bear any burden for God's honor, knowing that I am being used for that same honor. ....

You know that I must follow God's will, and I know that you want me to follow it. It was God's will that I go away—and my going was not without mystery, nor without worthwhile results. It was also God's will that I remain away; it was no mere human decision. ... You were glad, I remember, for the sake of material gain when your sons left home to win temporal wealth. But now when it is a question of winning eternal life it seems to be so hard that you say you are going to go to pieces if I don't answer you soon. All this because you love the part of me that I got from you (I mean your flesh, in which you clothed me) more than you love the part of me that I got from God. Lift, lift up your heart and affection a bit to that dear most holy cross, where every burden becomes light.

(LETTER 84)

O MARY,
      I see this Word given to you
yet not separated from the Father—
just as the word one has in one's mind
does not leave one's heart
or become separated from it
even though that word is externalized
and communicated to others . . .

(FROM PRAYER 18)

O GOD ETERNAL,
O good master!
You made and shaped the vessel of your crea-
    ture's body
from the clay of the earth.
O tenderest love!
Of such a lowly thing you shaped it,
and then you put within it
no less a treasure than the soul,
the soul that bears the image of you,
God eternal.
You, good master,
my sweet love—
you are the master who breaks and refashions;
you smash this vessel
and put it back together again
as it pleases your goodness.

To you, eternal Father,
I offer once again my life,
poor as I am,
for your dear bride.
As often as it pleases your goodness,
drag me out of this body
and send me back again,
each time with greater suffering than before,
if only I may see the reform
of this dear bride, holy Church.
I beg you, God eternal: give me this bride.

. . . I offer and commend to you my children,
whom I so love,
for they are my soul.
But should it please your goodness
to make me stay yet longer in this vessel,

then do you, best of doctors,
heal and care for it,
for it is all shattered.
Give,
O give to us, eternal Father,
your gentle benediction.
Amen.

(FROM PRAYER 26—
THE LAST RECORDED)

CHAPTER FIVE

Saint Catherine of Genoa

1447–1510

❦

AS A MARRIED WOMAN *and the administrator of a huge city hospital, Catherine of Genoa is that rare saint for whom contemporary women can feel a certain affinity.*

But in fact, this aristocratic young woman married under duress, and to someone hopelessly unsuited for her. Plunged at first into profound depression, she tried without success to lose herself in social activities. Finally, after ten years' struggle, she seems to have sensed that a change was coming. Pleading a mild illness, she withdrew into prayer and silence.

Three months later, March 22, 1473, Catherine's old life ended and a new one began. "I live no longer," she exulted, "but Christ lives in me." The sheer vehement force of her conversion catapulted her out of her palazzo and into the slums of Genoa, whose poor and destitute she would serve for the rest of her life.

The following selections are from *Life and Doctrine of Saint Catherine of Genoa,* translated by Mrs. George Ripley (New York: Christian Press Association Publishing, 1896), and from *Catherine of Genoa: Purgation and Purgatory, The Spiritual Dialogue,* translated by Serge Hughes (New York: Paulist Press, 1979).

*I*T APPEARED TO ME, as I noted from time to time, that the love wherewith I loved my sweet Love grew greater day by day, and yet, at each step, I had thought it as perfect as it could be, for love has this property that it can never perceive in itself the least defect. But as my vision grew clearer, I beheld in myself many imperfections which, had I seen them in the beginning, I should have esteemed nothing, not even hell itself, too great or painful that would have rid me of them. In the beginning they were hidden from me, for it was the purpose of God to accomplish his work by little and little, in order to keep me humble, and enable me to remain among my fellow creatures. And finally, seeing a completed work entirely beyond the creature, I am compelled to say what before I could not say, and confess how clear it is to me that all our works are even more imperfect than any creature can fully understand.

(*LIFE AND DOCTRINE* 49–50)

I SEE WITHOUT EYES, hear without understanding, feel without feeling, and taste without tasting. I know neither form nor measure; for without seeing I yet behold an operation so divine that the words I first used, perfection, purity, and the like, seem to me now mere lies in the presence of the truth. The sun which once looked so bright is now dark; what was sweet is now bitter, because sweetness and beauty are spoiled by contact with creatures. Nor can I any longer say: "My God, my All." Everything is mine, for all that is God's seems to be wholly mine. Neither in heaven nor on earth shall I ever again use such words, for I am mute and lost in God. . . .

(50)

I CANNOT DESIRE any created love, that is, love which can be felt, enjoyed, or understood. I do not wish love that can pass through the intellect, memory, or will; because pure love passes all these things and transcends them.

(66)

MY SELF IS GOD, nor is any other self known to me except my God.

(67)

WHEN THE GOOD GOD calls us in this world, he finds us full of vices and sins, and his first work is to give us the instinct to practice virtue; then he incites us to desire perfection, and afterwards, by infused grace, he conducts us to the true annihilation, and finally to the true transformation. This is the extraordinary road along which God conducts the soul. But when the soul is thus annihilated and transformed, it no longer works, or speaks, or wills, or feels, or understands, nor has it in itself any knowledge, either of that which is internal or external, which could possibly affect it; and in all these things God is its director and guide without the help of any creature.

In this state, the soul is in such peace and tranquillity that it seems to her that both soul and body are immersed in a sea of the profoundest peace, from which she would not issue for anything that could happen in this life. She remains immovable, imperturbable, and neither her humanity nor her spirit feels anything except the sweetest peace, of which she is so full, that if her flesh, her bones, her nerves were pressed, nothing would issue from them but peace. And all day long, she sings softly to herself for joy. . . .

(92)

IF I UTTERED a word, breathed a sigh, or cast a glance towards any person who could understand me, my humanity would be well content, as a thirsty person when given drink.

(139)

WHILE STILL IN THE FLESH this blessed soul [Catherine] experienced the fiery love of God, a love that consumed her, cleansing and purifying all, so that once quitted from this life she could appear forthwith in God's presence. As she dwelt on this love, the condition of the souls of the faithful in purgatory, where they are cleansed of the remaining rust and stain of sin, became clear to her.

(CATHERINE OF GENOA 71)

THERE IS NO JOY save that in paradise to be compared to the joy of the souls in purgatory. This joy increases day by day because of the way in which the love of God corresponds to that of the soul, since the impediment to that love is worn away daily. This impediment is the rust of sin. As it is consumed the soul is more and more open to God's love.

Just as a covered object left out in the sun cannot be penetrated by the sun's rays, in the same way, once the covering of the soul is removed, the soul opens itself fully to the rays of the sun. The more rust of sin is consumed by fire, the more the soul responds to that love, and its joy increases.

(72)

I AM MORE CONFUSED than satisfied with the words I have used to express myself, but I have found nothing better for what I have felt. All that I have said is as nothing compared to what I feel within, the witnessed correspondence of love between God and the Soul; for when God sees the Soul pure as it was in its origins, He tugs at it with a glance, draws it and binds it to Himself with a fiery love that by itself could annihilate the immortal soul. In so acting, God so transforms the soul in Him that it knows nothing other than God; and He continues to draw it up into His fiery love until He restores it to that pure state from which it first issued. As it is being drawn upwards, the soul feels itself melting in the fire of that love of its sweet God, for He will not cease until He has brought the soul to its perfection.

(79)

A ND I SEE RAYS of lightning darting from that divine love to the creature, so intense and fiery as to annihilate not the body alone but, were it possible, the soul. These rays purify and then annihilate. The soul becomes like gold that becomes purer as it is fired, all dross being cast out. This is the effect of fire on material things; but in this purification, what is obliterated and cast out is not the soul, one with God, but the lesser self. Having come to the point of twenty-four carats, gold cannot be purified any further; and this is what happens to the soul in the fire of God's love.

(79–80)

QUITE STILL and in a state of siege, the me within finds itself gradually stripped of all those things that in spiritual or bodily form gave it some comfort. And once the last of them has been removed the soul, understanding that they were at best supportive, turns its back on them completely.

(85)

SUCH KNOWLEDGE does not come through intellect or will, as I have said. It comes from God, with a rush. God busies the soul with Himself, in no matter how slight a way, and the soul, wrapped up in God, cannot but be oblivious to all else.

(87)

IN THIS WORLD, the rays of God's love, unbeknownst to man, encircle man all about, hungrily seeking to penetrate him.

(109)

*P*URE LOVE does not attach itself to pleasure or feeling, bodily or spiritual. In the same way, a spiritual attachment that seems good is dangerous. It can mislead the Soul into attaching itself not to God but to those pleasurable sentiments; he who seeks the naked love of God must flee these sentiments. Bodily sentiments, by contrast, are obviously opposed to the Spirit, and the appearance of being good is not as persuasive—that is why they are less dangerous. Spiritual pleasures, however, are something of a poison against pure love of God. They are more difficult to eradicate once we become attached to them. Not to understand this is to be barred from the one perfect good—God pure and naked.

(124)

A s for the spirit, I sense such peace and joy that it goes beyond words; with respect to humanity, the deepest suffering a body can feel is nothing to what I am experiencing.

(139)

N o more of this world, no more of this world!

(143)

CHAPTER SIX

Saint Teresa of Avila

1515–1582

❦

R EFORMER OF THE *Carmelite Order, Mother
Foundress of seventeen convents for Discalced
Carmelites, Teresa was named Doctor of the Church in
1970 along with Catherine of Siena. Her endearingly can-*

did autobiography is one of the few existing accounts of a female saint's life that deviates from the well-established norm of steady-state piety.

Witty, beautiful, lover of good books and intelligent conversation, this cloistered nun was held fast, suspended for nearly twenty years between "the things of God and the things of the world." It was mental prayer that enabled her finally to sever her last attachments to ordinary life and answer God's call wholeheartedly—and, indeed, no one explains mental prayer more vividly or penetratingly than this most unlikely of saints.

All of the excerpts are taken from the three-volume *Collected Works of St. Teresa of Avila* (Washington, DC: Institute of Carmelite Studies, 1976–85), except the two poems. These are translated by Eknath Easwaran and appear in his book of selected passages for meditation called *God Makes the Rivers to Flow* (Petaluma, CA: Nilgiri Press, 1982). I have designated chapter and section numbers of particular works rather than page numbers so that readers with other editions can easily find the passages in question.

*I*WAS LIVING an extremely burdensome life, because in prayer I understood more clearly my faults. On the one hand God was calling me; on the other hand I was following the world. All the things of God made me happy; those of the world held me bound. . . . In prayer I was having great trouble, for my spirit was not proceeding as lord but as slave. And so I was not able to shut myself within myself, as was my method of prayer. Instead, I shut within myself a thousand vanities.

(*LIFE* 7.17)

*I*VOYAGED ON THIS tempestuous sea for almost twenty years.

. . . When I was experiencing the enjoyments of the world, I felt sorrow when I recalled what I owed to God. When I was with God, my attachments to the world disturbed me. . . .

(8.2)

Mental prayer in my opinion is nothing else than an intimate sharing between friends; it means taking time frequently to be alone with Him who we know loves us.

(8.5)

THE BEGINNER must realize that in order to give delight to the Lord she is starting to cultivate a garden on very barren soil, full of abominable weeds. . . . It seems to me the garden can be watered in four ways. . . .

Beginners in prayer, we can say, are those who draw water from the well. This involves a lot of work on their own part, as I have said. They must tire themselves in trying to recollect their senses. Since they are accustomed to being distracted, this recollection requires much effort. . . .

(11.6–9)

L ET US SPEAK now of the second manner, ordained by the Lord of the garden, for getting water; that is, by turning the crank of a water wheel and by aqueducts, the gardener obtains more water with less labor; and he can rest without having to work constantly. Well, this method applied to what they call the prayer of quiet is what I now want to discuss.

Here the soul begins to be recollected and comes upon something supernatural, because in no way can it acquire this prayer through any effort it makes. . . .

This quiet and recollection is something that is clearly felt through the satisfaction and peace bestowed on the soul, along with great contentment and calm and a very gentle delight in the faculties. It seems to the soul, since it hasn't gone further, that there's nothing left to desire and that it should willingly say with St. Peter that it will make its dwelling there. It dares not move or stir, for it seems that good will slip through its hands—nor would it even want to breathe sometimes.

The poor little thing doesn't understand that since by its own efforts it can do nothing to draw that good to itself, so much less will it be able to keep it for longer than the Lord desires.

(14.1–2; 15.1, 4, 6)

LET US COME now to speak of the third water by which this garden is irrigated, that is, the water flowing from a river or spring. By this means the garden is irrigated with much less labor, although some labor is required to direct the flow of the water. The Lord so desires to help the gardener here that He Himself becomes practically the gardener and the one who does everything.

This prayer is a sleep of the faculties: the faculties neither fail entirely to function nor understand how they function. The consolation, the sweetness, and the delight are incomparably greater than that experienced in the previous prayer. The water of grace rises up to the throat of this soul since it can no longer move forward; nor does it know how; nor can it move backward. . . . It doesn't know whether to speak or to be silent, whether to laugh or to weep. This prayer is a glorious foolishness, a heavenly madness where the true wisdom is learned; and it is for the soul a most delightful way of enjoying. . . .

For in one of these visits, however brief, the water is given without measure because the gardener is who He is—in truth, the creator of the water. And what the poor soul could not achieve in about twenty years with its labors to bring repose to the intellect, this heavenly gardener accomplishes in a moment. And the fruit grows and matures in such a way that the soul can be sustained from its garden if the Lord so desires. But He doesn't give it permission to distribute fruit until it is very strong from what it has eaten. . . .

(16.1; 17.2, 4)

MAY THE LORD teach me the words necessary for explaining something about the fourth water. . . . Let us speak of this heavenly water that in its abundance soaks and saturates this entire garden. . . . While the soul is seeking God in this way, it feels with the most marvelous and gentlest delight that everything is almost fading away through a kind of swoon in which breathing and all the bodily energies gradually fail. . . . All the external energy is lost, and that of the soul is increased so that it might better enjoy its glory. . . .

After having received Communion and been in this very prayer I'm writing about, I was thinking when I wanted to write something on it of what the soul did during that time. The Lord spoke these words to me: "It detaches itself from everything, daughter, so as to abide more in me. It is no longer the soul that lives but I. Since it cannot comprehend what it understands, there is an understanding by not understanding." . . .

If the soil is well cultivated by trials, persecutions, criticisms, and illnesses—for few there must be who reach this stage without them—and if it is softened by living in great detachment from self-interest, the water soaks it to the extent that it is almost never dry. But if the soil is still hardened in the earth and has a lot of briars, as I did in the beginning, and is still not so removed from occasions and if it doesn't have the gratitude a favor as great as this deserves, the ground will dry up again. And if the gardener becomes careless and the Lord solely out of His goodness does not desire to let the rains come again, the garden can be considered as lost. So it happened to me sometimes. . . . I write this for the consolation of weak souls like myself. . . . Even though they may fall after elevations like the ones to which the Lord here brings them, they ought not to grow discouraged if they don't want to become completely lost. For tears gain all things; one water draws down the other.

(18.1, 9, 10, 14; 19.3)

THIS IS ANOTHER, new book from here on—I mean another, new life. The life dealt with up to this point was mine; the one I lived from the point where I began to explain these things about prayer is the one God lived in me—according to the way it appears to me—because I think it would have been impossible in so short a time to get rid of so many bad habits and deeds. May the Lord be praised who freed me from myself. . . . When I began to avoid occasions and devote myself to prayer, the Lord . . . started to grant me favors.

(23.1, 2)

SHOULD ANYONE tell you that prayer is dangerous, consider him the real danger and run from him.

(*WAY OF PERFECTION* 21.7)

THEN, DAUGHTERS, since you are alone, strive to find a companion. . . . Represent the Lord Himself as close to you and behold how lovingly and humbly

He is teaching you. Believe me, you should remain with so good a friend as long as you can. If you grow accustomed to having Him present at your side, and He sees that you do so with love and that you go about striving to please Him, you will not be able—as they say—to get away from Him; He will never fail you; He will help you in all your trials; you will find Him everywhere.

(26.1)

[On recollection:]

IF WE MAKE the effort, practice this recollection for some days, and get used to it, the gain will be clearly seen; we will understand, when beginning to pray, that the bees are approaching and entering the beehive to make honey. And this recollection will be effected without our effort because the Lord has desired that, during the time the faculties are drawn inward, the soul and its will may merit to have this dominion. When the soul does no more than give a sign that it wishes to be recollected, the senses obey it and become recollected. Even though they go out again afterward, their having already surrendered is a great thing; for they go out as captives and subjects and do not cause the harm they did previously. And when the will calls them back again, they come more quickly, until after many of these entries the Lord wills that they rest entirely in perfect contemplation.

(29.7)

[On the prayer of quiet:]

THE SOUL IS LIKE an infant that still nurses when at its mother's breast, and the mother without her babe's effort to suckle puts the milk in its mouth in order to give it delight. So it is here; for without effort of the intellect the will is loving, and the Lord desires that the will, without thinking about the matter, understand that it is with Him and that it does no more than swallow the milk His Majesty places in its mouth, and enjoy that sweetness. . . .

(31.9)

TODAY WHILE BESEECHING our Lord to speak for me because I wasn't able to think of anything to say nor did I know how to begin to carry out this obedience, there came to my mind what I shall now speak about. . . . It is that we consider our soul to be like a castle made entirely out of a diamond or of very clear crystal, in which there are many rooms, just as in heaven there are many dwelling places. . . .

You mustn't think of these dwelling places in such a way that each one would follow in file after the other; but turn your eyes toward the center, which is the room or royal chamber where the King stays, and think of how a palmetto has many leaves surrounding and covering the tasty part that can be eaten. So here, surrounding this center room are many other rooms; and the same holds true for those above. The things of the soul must always be considered as plentiful, spacious, and large. . . . The soul is capable of much more than we can imagine, and the sun that is in this royal chamber shines in all parts. It is very important for any soul that practices prayer, whether little or much, not to hold itself back and stay in one corner. Let it walk through these dwelling places which are up above, down below, and to the sides, since God has given it such great dignity. . . .

(*INTERIOR CASTLE* 1.1.1; 1.2.8)

DOING OUR OWN will is usually what harms us.

(3.2.12)

THE IMPORTANT THING is not to think much but to love much; and so do that which best stirs you to love. Perhaps we don't know what love is. I wouldn't be very surprised, because it doesn't consist in great delight but in desiring with strong determination to please God in everything. . . . Don't think the matter lies in thinking of nothing else, and that if you become a little distracted all is lost.

(4.1.8)

IT SEEMS THAT since that heavenly water begins to rise from this spring I'm mentioning that is deep within us, it swells and expands our whole interior being, producing ineffable blessings; nor does the soul even understand what is given to it there. It perceives a fragrance, let us say for now, as though there were in that interior depth a brazier giving off sweet-smelling perfumes. No light is seen, nor is the place seen where the brazier is; but the warmth and the fragrant fumes spread through the entire soul and even often enough, as I have said, the body shares in them. See now that you understand me; no heat is felt, nor is there the scent of any perfume, for the experience is more delicate than an experience of these things; but I use the examples only so as to explain it to you.

(4.2.6)

FOR INDEED THE SOUL does no more in this union than does the wax when another impresses a seal on it. The wax doesn't impress the seal upon itself; it is only disposed—I mean, by being soft. And even in order to be disposed, it doesn't soften itself but remains still and gives its consent.

(5.2.14)

. . . Union is like the joining of two wax candles to such an extent that the flame coming from them is but one . . . but afterward one candle can be easily separated from the other and there are two candles. . . . In the spiritual marriage the union is like what we have when rain falls from the sky into a river or fount; all is water. . . .

. . . There is a great detachment from everything and a desire to be always either alone or occupied in something that will benefit some soul. There are no interior trials or feelings of dryness, but the soul lives with a remembrance and tender love of our Lord. . . .

All its concern is taken up with how to please Him more and how or where it will show Him the love it bears Him. This is the reason for prayer, my daughters, the purpose of this spiritual marriage: the birth always of good works, good works. . . .

Sometimes the devil gives us great desires so that we will avoid setting ourselves to the task at hand, serving our Lord in possible things, and instead be content with having desired the impossible. . . . The Lord doesn't so much look at the greatness of our works as at the love with which they are done.

(7.2.4; 7.3.8; 7.4.6, 14–15)

*W*ELL, COME NOW, my daughters, don't be sad when obedience draws you to involvement in exterior matters. Know that if it is in the kitchen, the Lord walks among the pots and pans helping you both interiorly and exteriorly. . . .

Here, my daughters, is where love will be seen: not hidden in corners but in the midst of the occasions of falling.

(*FOUNDATIONS* 5.8, 15)

*H*ER HEART is full of joy with love,
For in the Lord her mind is stilled.
She has renounced every selfish attachment
And draws abiding joy and strength from the
  One within.
She lives not for herself, but lives
To serve the Lord of Love in all,

And swims across the sea of life
breasting its rough waves joyfully.

(GOD MAKES THE RIVERS TO FLOW 30)

L ET NOTHING upset you,
Let nothing frighten you.
Everything is changing;
God alone is changeless.
Patience attains the goal.
Who has God lacks nothing;
God alone fills all his needs.

(30)

ACKNOWLEDGMENTS

Reprinted from St. Hildegard of Bingen: *Symphonia: A Critical Edition of the Symphonia armonie celestium revelationum.* Edited and translated by Barbara Newman. Copyright © 1989 by Cornell University. Used by permission of the publisher, Cornell University Press.

Reprinted from *Julian of Norwich: Showings,* translated by Edmund Colledge, O.S.A. and James Walsh, S.J. Copyright © 1978 by The Missionary Society of St. Paul the Apostle in the State of New York. Used by permission of Paulist Press.

Reprinted from *Catherine of Siena: The Dialogue,* translated by Suzanne Noffke, O.P. Copyright © 1980 by The Missionary Society of St. Paul the Apostle in the State of New York. Used by permission of Paulist Press.

Reprinted from *Hildegard of Bingen: Scivias,* translated by Mother Columba Hart and Jane Bishop. Copyright © 1990 by the Abbey of Regina Laudis: Benedictine Congregation Regina Laudis of the Strict Observance, Inc. Used by permission of Paulist Press.

Reprinted from *Catherine of Genoa: Purgation and Purgatory, The Spiritual Dialogue,* translated by Serge Hughes. Copyright © 1979 by The Missionary Society of St. Paul the Apostle in the State of New York. Used by permission of Paulist Press.